Usborne
Christmas
Baking
for
Children

Fiona Patchett

Illustrated by Nancy Leschnikoff

Designed by Nelupa Hussain

Recipe consultants: Catherine Atkinson and Dagmar Vesely

Contents

Allergy-free recipes

Ⓦ wheat-free   Ⓖ gluten-free

Ⓓ dairy-free   Ⓔ egg-free

Ⓝ contains nuts

Recipes marked with a ✳ have special instructions you will need to follow to make them allergy-free.

Getting started

Before you start cooking, read through the following few pages for some basic baking skills. Then read the recipe, check you have all the ingredients and equipment you need and get baking.

Weighing and measuring

It's important that you measure things out exactly and don't leave anything out, otherwise your cakes and biscuits might not turn out quite right.

Weigh dry ingredients on kitchen scales and measure liquids in a measuring jug. For small amounts, use measuring spoons if you can, but normal spoons will do.

When you measure out a spoonful, the ingredient should lie level with the top of the spoon.

Always use the size and shape of tin suggested in the recipe.

Your oven

Bake things on the middle shelf of your oven. If you have a fan oven, you may need to lower the temperature or shorten cooking times. Check your oven's manual.

Don't open the oven door while you're cooking, unless the recipe tells you to, or if you think something might be burning. Remember to put on oven gloves before you pick up anything hot.

Keeping clean

You'll find it much easier if you try to clean up as you go along. Put things away after you've used them. If you spill anything, wipe it up straight away. And always wash your hands before you start.

If the recipe lists softened butter, take it out of the fridge 30 minutes before you use it.

Baking skills

There are many simple skills that cooks use when they are baking. Here are some that will help you make the recipes in this book.

Breaking an egg

Crack the shell sharply on the edge of a bowl. Push your thumbs into the crack and pull the shell apart, so the egg falls into the bowl.

Beating eggs

Use a fork.

Stir the eggs quickly to mix the whites and yolks together.

Separating eggs

Break an egg onto a plate. Cover the yolk with an egg cup and hold it, while you tip the plate so the white slides off.

Whisking egg whites

①

Pour the egg whites into a clean, dry bowl, making sure no yolk gets in. Hold the bowl tightly.

② Move the whisk quickly around and around in the bowl. Carry on until stiff points or 'peaks' form on top, when you lift the whisk, like this.

Grating

Be careful not to scrape your fingers.

Hold the food you are grating firmly. Scrape it across the holes again and again. Use the small holes for orange or lemon zest.

Squeezing

Cut the fruit in half. Press one half at a time onto a citrus squeezer. Twist as you press.

Sifting

Put the icing sugar, flour or cocoa in a sieve over a bowl. Shake the sieve.

Beating a mixture

Stir the mixture quickly with a wooden spoon. Carry on until the mixture is smooth.

Folding in

Slice through the ingredients with a metal spoon and gently turn them over and over until they are evenly mixed.

Rubbing in

Use your fingers to rub the butter into the flour. Lift the mixture and let it fall back into the bowl as you rub. Carry on until the mixture looks like fine breadcrumbs.

Rolling out

① Put the dough onto a clean, dry surface. Press the rolling pin onto it and roll away from you.

Dust the surface and rolling pin with flour.

② Turn the dough around a little and roll again. Carry on until the dough is the thickness you need.

Greasing and lining

To grease a tin, dip a paper towel into some softened butter or cooking oil. Rub it over the inside of the tin.

To line a tin, put it on some baking parchment. Draw around it with a pencil. Cut just inside the line. Lay the parchment in the tin.

Turning out cakes

① When the tin is cool, run a knife around the sides of the tin. Choose a plate slightly larger than the tin and hold it over the tin.

② Turn the tin and plate over together, so the cake turns out onto the plate. Then, lift the tin off the cake.

Christmas cookies

These vanilla cookies are very simple to make. Cut them into Christmas shapes and decorate them with icing and sugar sprinkles.

Ingredients:

125g (4½oz) butter, softened

50g (2oz) icing sugar

1 medium egg

1 teaspoon vanilla extract

225g (8oz) plain flour

For the icing:

225g (8oz) icing sugar

2½ tablespoons warm water

You will also need:

some shaped cookie cutters

sugar sprinkles to decorate

❄ Makes around 35 cookies.

1 First, grease two baking trays. Then, put the butter in a large bowl. Beat it until it is smooth. Use a sieve to sift in the icing sugar. Beat again.

2 Break the egg into a small bowl. Add the vanilla extract and beat well with a fork.

3 Add the eggy mixture to the large bowl, a little at a time. Beat well between each addition.

Dust the surface and a rolling pin with flour.

4 Add the flour and stir the mixture until it starts to form a dough. Then, use your hands to mix the dough and squeeze it into a ball.

5 Wrap the dough in plastic foodwrap and put it in the fridge for 30 minutes. Heat the oven to 180°C, 350°F or gas mark 4.

6 Unwrap the dough and put it onto a clean surface. Roll it out until it is just thinner than your little finger. Use the cutters to cut out lots of shapes.

7

Put the cookies onto the trays. Squeeze the scraps together and roll them out again. Cut out more shapes and put them on the trays.

8

Bake for 10-12 minutes until golden. Leave on the trays for 5 minutes, then put on a wire rack to cool.

9

For the icing, sift the icing sugar into a bowl and mix it with the warm water. Spread onto each cookie with a blunt knife. Scatter sugar sprinkles on top.

These will keep for up to 5 days in an airtight container.

You could add different flavours to your cookies. Here are some suggestions. Leave out the vanilla and, at step 4, add:

✻ 1 teaspoon of ground cardamom or cinnamon

✻ 2 teaspoons of ground ginger or orange zest

Lemon cinnamon stars

These delicious and chewy biscuits are flavoured with cinnamon and lemon.
They are popular in Switzerland, Austria and Germany, where they
are known as 'Zimtsterne', meaning cinnamon stars.

Ingredients:

2 lemons

250g (9oz) icing sugar

400g (14oz) ground almonds

2 teaspoons ground cinnamon

2 medium eggs

For the lemon icing:

125g (4^1/$_2$oz) icing sugar

1^1/$_2$ tablespoons lemon juice

You will also need:

a small star-shaped cutter

❄ Makes around 40 stars.

① Heat the oven to 200°C, 400°F or gas mark 6. Line a baking tray. Grate the zest from the lemons.

② Sift the icing sugar into a large bowl. Mix it with the lemon zest, ground almonds and cinnamon.

You don't need the yolks.

③ Separate the eggs. Put the whites into a large, clean bowl. Whisk them until they are really thick. They should make stiff peaks, like this.

④ Gently fold the almond mixture into the egg whites to make a stiff dough. If it's too sticky, add more ground almonds.

Dust the surface and rolling pin with icing sugar.

⑤ Put the dough onto a work surface and roll it out until it is as thick as your little finger.

⑥ Use the cutter to cut out star shapes and put them on the baking tray.

You could decorate
these biscuits with
lemon zest. Use a zester
to get long curls of zest.

⑦ Bake for 5-6 minutes.
Leave on the tray for
a few minutes, then
put them on a wire
rack to cool.

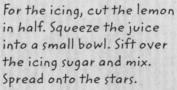

⑧ For the icing, cut the lemon
in half. Squeeze the juice
into a small bowl. Sift over
the icing sugar and mix.
Spread onto the stars.

These will keep
for up to 5 days
in an airtight
container.

Shortbread

Shortbread was traditionally eaten in Scotland at New Year, and the round shape was supposed to look like the sun. But now, shortbread is popular all year, around the world.

Ingredients:

150g (5oz) plain flour

25g (1oz) ground rice or rice flour

100g (4oz) butter, chilled

50g (2oz) caster sugar

100g (4oz) white chocolate

sugar stars to decorate (optional)

You will also need:
a 20cm (8in) round tin

❄ Makes 8 slices.

1. Heat the oven to 150°C, 300°F or gas mark 2. Grease the tin. Mix the flour and ground rice in a large bowl.

2. Cut the butter into chunks. Rub it into the flour until the mixture looks like fine breadcrumbs. Stir in the sugar.

3. Squeeze the mixture into a ball. The heat from your hands makes the dough stick together.

4. Press the mixture into the tin with your fingers. Use the back of a spoon to smooth the top and make it level.

5. Use a fork to press a pattern around the edge. Then, cut the mixture into 8 equal pieces.

6. Bake for 30 minutes until golden. Leave in the tin for 5 minutes. Then cut across it again and put the pieces on a wire rack to cool.

7

Pour some water into a pan, so it's about 3cm (1in) deep. Heat until it bubbles, then turn off the heat.

8

Put the chocolate in a heatproof bowl. Carefully put it into the pan. Stir the chocolate until it melts. Lift the bowl out of the pan.

9

Dip each piece of shortbread into the chocolate, then put it onto a sheet of baking parchment on a plate. Put in the fridge for 20 minutes to set.

You could decorate your shortbread with bought sugar stars.

This will keep for up to 5 days in an airtight container.

Chocolate orange hearts

When you bite into these crispy chocolate hearts, you'll find a rich orange filling inside.

Ingredients:

100g (4oz) self-raising flour
25g (1oz) cocoa powder
75g (3oz) butter, chilled
50g (2oz) caster sugar
1 medium egg

For the orange filling:
50g (2oz) caster sugar

50g (2oz) ground almonds
2 oranges

You will also need:

a heart-shaped cutter,
    at least 5cm (2in) across

❈ Makes around 15 biscuits.

1 Grease a baking tray. Mix the flour and cocoa in a large bowl. Cut the butter into chunks and add it to the mixture.

2 Rub the butter into the flour until it looks like breadcrumbs. Stir in the sugar. Separate the egg and stir in the yolk. Put the egg white in a cup to use later.

3 Squeeze everything together to make a ball of dough. Wrap it in foodwrap. Put it in the fridge for 20 minutes.

4 For the filling, put half the egg white in a bowl with the sugar and ground almonds.

5 Grate the zest from the oranges. Add it to the bowl and mix everything together well.

Dust your hands with icing sugar.

6 Take a teaspoon of the mixture. Roll it into a ball, then flatten it slightly. Make 15 balls. Heat the oven to 200°C, 400°F or gas mark 6.

Dust the rolling pin and surface with icing sugar.

7

Take the dough out of the fridge. Roll it out until it is as thick as your little finger. Press hard as you roll.

8

Cut out 30 hearts. Put half on the tray. Put a ball of filling on each one. Brush the edges with egg white. Put a second heart on top and press the edges together.

9

Bake for 8-10 minutes. Leave on the tray for a few minutes, then put on a wire rack to cool.

These chocolate orange hearts look pretty if you sift a little icing sugar over them.

These will keep for up to 5 days in an airtight container.

Stained-glass windows

These biscuits look lovely with light shining through them. You could decorate them with icing or writing icing, and hang them on a Christmas tree.

Ingredients:

50g (2oz) soft light brown sugar

50g (2oz) butter, softened

1 small egg

115g (4½oz) plain flour

15g (½oz) cornflour

1 teaspoon mixed spice

20 see-through boiled sweets

You will also need:

a large shaped cookie cutter
  (stars or snowflakes look good)

a drinking straw

a small round cutter, slightly bigger
  than the sweets

❄ Makes around 20 biscuits.

①
Heat the oven to 180°C, 350°F or gas mark 4. Grease and line a baking tray.

②
Beat the sugar and butter in a large bowl. Break the egg into a small bowl and beat it. Mix half the egg into the butter and sugar. You don't need the other half.

③
Stir in the flour, cornflour and mixed spice. Mix everything together really well.

④
Squeeze the mixture together with your hands to form a ball of dough.

Dust the surface and rolling pin with flour.

⑤
Roll out the dough until it is as thick as your little finger. Use the large cutter to cut out shapes. Lift them onto the tray with a spatula.

⑥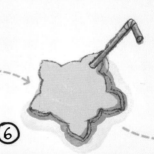
Make a hole in each biscuit by pressing the straw through the dough, near the top of each one.

To decorate your biscuits, you could cover them with icing (see page 44) or draw on patterns with writing icing. If you're going to hang them up, leave them to dry first and don't eat them afterwards — they might be dirty.

These will keep for up to 4 days in an airtight container.

⑦ Use the small, round cutter to cut a hole in the middle of each biscuit.

⑧ Squeeze the scraps together and roll them out again. Cut out more biscuits.

⑨ Put a sweet into the hole in the middle of each biscuit. Bake for 12 minutes. Leave on the tray until they are cold.

Linz biscuits

These delicious hazelnut biscuits are from the city of Linz in Austria. They have a shaped hole cut in the top so the raspberry jam filling shows through.

Ingredients:

100g (4oz) hazelnuts

200g (7oz) plain flour

150g (5oz) caster sugar

150g (5oz) butter, chilled

1 medium egg

1/2 teaspoon vanilla essence

raspberry jam (or any flavour)

You will also need:

a 6cm (2¹/₂in) round cutter

small cutters in different shapes

❄ Makes around 14 biscuits.

① Put the nuts into a plastic food bag and seal the end. Use a rolling pin to crush them into small pieces.

② Put the nuts, flour and sugar into a large bowl. Cut the butter into chunks and rub it into the flour until it looks like breadcrumbs.

③ Separate the egg. Put the yolk into the bowl and add the vanilla essence. Mix everything together until it forms a dough.

④ Wrap the dough in foodwrap. Put it in the fridge to chill for 30 minutes.

Dust the surface and rolling pin with flour.

⑤ Heat the oven to 200°C, 400°F or gas mark 6. Line two baking trays with baking parchment. Then, roll out the dough until it is as thick as your little finger.

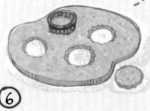

⑥ Use the round cutter to cut out lots of circles. Squeeze the scraps into a ball. Roll it out and cut more circles.

(7) Use the small cutter to cut holes in half of the circles. Put all the circles onto the trays and bake for 8 minutes.

(8) Take the biscuits out of the oven. Leave them on the tray for 2 minutes, then put them on a wire rack to cool.

(9) Spread jam on the whole biscuits, as far as the edge. Place a cut-out biscuit on each one and press it down gently.

These will keep for up to 5 days in an airtight container.

Mince pies

Mince pies have been a Christmas treat in Britain for centuries. Mincemeat used to contain real meat as well as fruit, but now it's made from fruits and spices. Some people put out a mince pie on Christmas Eve to thank Father Christmas for their presents.

Ingredients:

For the mincemeat:

1 orange

1 lemon

75g (3oz) seedless grapes

25g (1oz) hazelnuts (optional)

1 apple

150g (5oz) raisins

ground cinnamon, nutmeg and ginger

For the orange pastry:

1 medium orange

1 medium egg

175g (6oz) plain flour

35g (1¼oz) icing sugar

100g (4oz) butter

You will also need:

a 12-hole bun tray

a 6½cm (2½in) round cutter

a 5cm (2in) round cutter

a small shaped cutter

❄ Makes 12 mince pies.

These will keep for up to 3 days in an airtight container.

①

Follow the steps on page 43 to make the mincemeat. For the pastry, grate the zest from the orange. Then squeeze the juice from half the orange.

Save the egg white to use later.

② Separate the egg and put the yolk into a small bowl. Mix in the zest and two teaspoons of orange juice.

③

Put the flour and sugar into a large bowl. Cut the butter into chunks and rub it into the flour, until it looks like fine breadcrumbs.

You can buy mincemeat if you don't want to make your own.

④

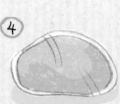

Stir in the orange mixture to make the dough. Wrap in foodwrap and put in the fridge for 30 minutes. Heat the oven to 190°C, 375°F or gas mark 5.

Dust the surface and rolling pin with flour.

⑤

Put the pastry onto a clean surface. Roll over it once. Turn it a quarter of the way around and roll over it again. Carry on until it's as thick as your little finger.

⑥

Use the large round cutter to cut out 12 circles. Put one in each hole in the tray. Squeeze the scraps together and roll them out. Use the small round cutter to cut 6 lids.

⑦

Use the shaped cutter to cut holes in the 6 lids. Then, spoon a heaped teaspoon of mincemeat into each pastry case.

⑧

Put lids with cut-out shapes onto half the pies. Put the small shapes on the others. Brush the pastry with the egg white you saved.

⑨

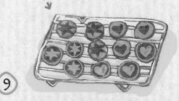

Bake for 20 minutes until golden. Leave in the tin for a few minutes. Then, put them on a wire rack to cool.

White chocolate brownies

Made with white chocolate and tangy cranberries, these brownies are a pale and interesting alternative to traditional brownies. Crispy on top and gooey inside, they are good eaten while they are still slightly warm.

Ingredients:

200g (7oz) white chocolate drops

75g (3oz) butter

3 medium eggs

175g (6oz) caster sugar

1 teaspoon vanilla essence

175g (6oz) plain flour

pinch of salt

75g (3oz) dried cranberries

You will also need:

a 20cm (8in) square cake tin

❄ Makes around 25 squares.

These will keep for up to 4 days in an airtight container.

① Heat the oven to 180°C, 350°F or gas mark 4. Grease and line the tin. Pour 5cm (2in) of water into a pan and heat it gently. When it bubbles, take it off the heat.

② Put half the chocolate drops into a heatproof bowl with the butter, cut into chunks. Carefully, put the bowl into the pan.

③ Stir until the butter and chocolate have melted. Lift the bowl out of the pan.

④ Beat the eggs in a large bowl. Stir in the sugar and vanilla essence. Add the chocolate mixture a little at a time, beating well between each addition.

⑤ Fold in the flour, salt, cranberries and the rest of the chocolate drops.

⑥ Spoon the mixture into the tin. Bake for 25 minutes for soft, gooey brownies, or 30 minutes to make them firmer.

⑦ Leave in the tin for 20 minutes. Then, cut into little squares. Sift icing sugar over the top, if you like.

You could add different ingredients to your brownies, instead of cranberries. Here are some suggestions. At step 5, try adding:

❋ chopped crystallized ginger

❋ tiny cubes of marzipan

❋ mini marshmallows

❋ chopped macadamia nuts, hazelnuts, pecans or walnuts

❋ plain or milk chocolate drops or chunks

Christmas cupcakes

These pretty cupcakes are drizzled with the juice of Christmassy clementines, then covered with a layer of white icing.

Ingredients:

For the cupcakes:

3 clementines

90g (3^1/$_2$oz) caster sugar

90g (3^1/$_2$oz) butter, softened

2 medium eggs

90g (3^1/$_2$oz) self-raising flour

For the icing:

175g (6oz) icing sugar

1^1/$_2$ tablespoons warm water

You will also need:

a 12-hole shallow bun tray

12 paper cupcake cases

❄ Makes 12 cupcakes.

① Heat the oven to 190°C, 375°F or gas mark 5. Put a paper case in each hole in the tray. Grate the zest from the clementines.

② Beat the sugar, butter and zest in a large bowl. Break the eggs into a cup. Add the eggs and flour to the bowl. Beat until everything is well mixed.

③ Use a teaspoon to divide the mixture between the cases. Bake for 15 minutes until risen and firm.

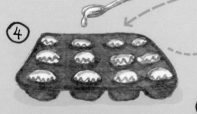

④ Squeeze the juice from the clementines. Spoon it over the cakes while they are still warm.

⑤ Put the cakes on a wire rack. Leave them until they are cool, then make the icing.

⑥ Sift the icing sugar into a bowl and mix it with the warm water. Spread onto each cake with a blunt knife.

These will
keep for up
to 4 days in
an airtight
container.

You could decorate
your cupcakes with
holly leaves and berries
made from marzipan or
ready-to-roll icing. Find
out how on page 45.

Spiced apple muffins

These apple muffins will fill your kitchen with the Christmassy smells of cinnamon, cloves, orange and lemon.

Ingredients:

3 eating apples

100g (4oz) butter

3 cloves

250g (9oz) self-raising flour

1$\frac{1}{2}$ teaspoons baking powder

1$\frac{1}{2}$ teaspoons ground cinnamon

25g (1oz) cornflour

200g (7oz) caster sugar

2 medium eggs

175ml (6fl oz) milk

For the topping:

1 small lemon

1 small orange

50g (2oz) demerara sugar

You will also need:

a 12-hole muffin tray

12 muffin cases (see page 46 to find out how to make your own)

❄ Makes 12 muffins.

1 Heat the oven to 190°C, 375°F or gas mark 5. Put a paper case in each hole in the tray.

Make sure the knife is facing away from you.

2 Use a peeler to peel the skin off an apple. Cut it into quarters. Put them on a board. Make two cuts in each one, in a V-shape, to cut out the core. Then, cut the quarters into chunks.

Stir every now and then.

3 Do the same with the other apples. Put them in a pan with the butter and cloves. Cook over a low heat for 5 minutes. Turn off the heat.

4 In a large bowl, mix the flour, baking powder, cinnamon, cornflour and sugar. Beat the eggs and milk in a jug.

5 Use a wooden spoon to remove the cloves from the pan. Pour the apple mixture and the eggy mixture into the flour.

6 Stir until everything is just mixed. It should still look quite lumpy.

24

7

Spoon the mixture into the paper cases. Bake for 18-20 minutes until firm and golden.

8

Squeeze the juice from half the lemon and half the orange, and mix it with the sugar. Spoon over the muffins while they're still hot.

At step 4, you could add some of these if you like:

✳ a handful of raisins or dried cranberries

✳ a few chopped walnuts or hazelnuts

These will keep for up to 2 days in an airtight container.

Mini Christmas cakes

These little square Christmas cakes are packed with fruit. First, make one big cake, decorate it with marzipan and icing, then cut it into 25 mini cakes.

Ingredients:

125g (4½oz) butter, softened

125g (4½oz) dark muscovado sugar

2 large eggs

1 orange

1 lemon

200g (7oz) mixture of dried figs, prunes, apricots and dates

50g (2oz) mixture of dried cranberries and glacé cherries

250g (9oz) mixture of currants, raisins and sultanas

25g (1oz) chopped mixed peel

125g (4½oz) plain flour

½ teaspoon baking powder

2 teaspoons mixed spice

To decorate:

2 tablespoons smooth apricot jam

400g (14oz) marzipan (optional)

400g (14oz) icing sugar

4 tablespoons warm water

You will also need:

a 20cm (8in) square cake tin

❄ Makes 25 mini cakes.

1

Heat the oven to 180°C, 350°F or gas mark 4. Line the tin with parchment. Cut another square of parchment the same size to use later.

2

Cut two strips of parchment 35cm (14in) long and 12cm (5in) wide. Use the strips to line the sides of the tin.

3

The mixture will look lumpy.

Beat the butter and sugar in a large bowl. Beat the eggs in a cup, then add them to the bowl a little at a time, beating well between each addition.

4

Grate the zest from the orange and lemon. Squeeze the juice from the orange. Add the zest and juice to the mixture.

5

Remove the date stones if there are any. Use scissors to snip the figs, prunes, apricots and dates into small pieces. Add the fruit to the bowl.

6

Add the cranberries, cherries, currants, raisins, sultanas, mixed peel, flour, baking powder and mixed spice. Mix everything together well.

You could decorate each cake with a glacé cherry. For more decorating ideas see pages 44-45.

These will keep for up to a month in an airtight container.

7

Spoon the mixture into the tin. Use the spoon to push it into the corners and smooth the top. Lay the square of parchment on top.

8

Bake for 50 minutes to an hour. Peel off the parchment. Push a skewer into the cake. If it comes out without cake stuck to it, it's ready.

9

Leave the cake in the tin until it's cool. Turn it onto a wire rack. Peel off the parchment. Spread jam over the cake.

10

Roll out the marzipan until it is bigger than the cake. Fold it over the rolling pin and lift it onto the cake.

11

Use scissors to trim the edges off the marzipan. For the icing, sift the icing sugar into a bowl. Mix with the water. Spread over the cake.

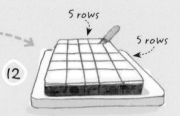

5 rows

5 rows

12

Leave the icing to dry, then cut into 25 squares, using a sharp knife.

Ⓡ ✱ You can replace the butter with dairy-free spread and the milk with soya or lactose-free milk.

Kringle

This festive Danish bread is flavoured with lemon and cardamom, and filled with cinnamon butter.

Ingredients:

8 cardamom pods

2 lemons

350g (12oz) strong white bread flour

1/2 teaspoon salt

25g (1oz) caster sugar

2 teaspoons fast action yeast

50g (2oz) butter

150ml (1/4 pint) milk

1 medium egg

For the cinnamon filling:

50g (2oz) butter, softened

50g (2oz) caster sugar

2 teaspoons ground cinnamon

1

Snip open the cardamom pods. Crush the seeds with a rolling pin. Grate the zest from the lemons. Mix the seeds, zest, flour, salt, sugar and yeast in a large bowl.

2

Heat the butter and half the milk in a pan until the butter has melted. Turn off the heat.

3

Beat the egg with the rest of the milk in a jug. Put a tablespoonful in a cup for later.

4

Add the eggy mixture and the buttery mixture to the flour. Stir to make a dough.

5

To knead the dough, press the heels of both hands into it. Push it away from you firmly. Fold it in half and turn it around.

6

Carry on pushing the dough away from you, folding it and turning it around for 10 minutes, until it feels smooth and springy.

This kringle is decorated with a drizzle of lemon icing (see page 44) and some chopped glacé cherries and pistachio nuts.

This will keep for up to 4 days in an airtight container.

7

It doesn't matter if the edges are wavy.

Roll the dough into a sausage about 40cm (16in) long. Flatten it with rolling pin, so it is about 15cm (6in) wide.

8

For the filling, beat the butter, sugar and cinnamon in a bowl. Spread over the dough, leaving a 2cm (¾in) border around the edge.

9

Brush water along one long edge. Roll up the dough from the other long edge. Press firmly along the join.

10

Put it onto a baking tray with the join facing down. Shape into a large knot, tucking both ends under. Cover with a clean tea towel.

11

Leave in a warm place for 1-2 hours until it has risen to twice its original size. Heat the oven to 200°C, 400°F or gas mark 6.

12

Take off the towel. Brush the dough with the eggy mixture you set aside. Bake for 25-30 minutes until golden. Put onto a wire rack to cool.

W S D N * See page 31 for an allergy-free version.

Christmas log

Christmas log is popular in France, where it is known as 'bûche de Noël'. Traditionally, at midwinter celebrations, a huge log was brought inside and burned on the fire. Christmas log is often decorated to look like a real log.

Ingredients:

4 large eggs
125g (4½oz) caster sugar
60g (2½oz) ground almonds
2½ tablespoons cocoa powder
1¼ teaspoons baking powder

For the chocolate buttercream:
100g (4oz) butter, softened
225g (8oz) icing sugar

1 tablespoon warm water
1 tablespoon cocoa powder

For the raspberry cream filling:
200ml (7fl oz) whipping cream
150g (5oz) fresh raspberries
1½ tablespoons caster sugar

You will also need:
a 35 x 25cm (14 x 10in) Swiss roll tin

1

Heat the oven to 180°C, 350°F or gas mark 4. Grease and line the tin. Separate the eggs so the whites are in one bowl and the yolks are in another.

2

Beat the sugar with the yolks until they are pale and thick. Stir in the ground almonds, cocoa and baking powder.

3

Using a whisk, whisk the egg whites, until they are really thick. When you lift up the whisk, they should make stiff peaks, like this.

4

Gently fold the whites into the yolk mixture. Pour into the tin. Bake for 20-25 minutes until firm.

5

Then, leave the cake in the tin for ten minutes. Cover it with a clean tea towel. Put it in the fridge for an hour.

6

For the buttercream, beat the butter and icing sugar in a bowl until they are smooth. Mix the water and cocoa. Stir them into the buttercream.

7 For the filling, whip the cream (see page 42). Mash the raspberries with a fork. Stir them into the cream, with the sugar.

8 Take the cake out of the fridge. Run a knife around the edges. Sift some icing sugar onto a surface and turn the cake onto it.

9 Peel the parchment off the top of the cake. Spread the filling over the cake. Carefully roll it up from one of the short ends. Lift it onto a plate.

10 Spread the chocolate buttercream all over the cake.

(see page 42)

This will keep for up to 3 days in the fridge, in an airtight container.

* For a dairy-free version, use dairy-free spread instead of butter. For the filling, mix 150g (5oz) fresh raspberries with 2 tablespoons raspberry jam (check the jam is dairy-free).

* To make it gluten-free and wheat-free, use gluten-free and wheat-free baking powder.

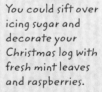

You could sift over icing sugar and decorate your Christmas log with fresh mint leaves and raspberries.

Maple syrup cupcakes

These cupcakes are flavoured with maple syrup and topped with a swirl of buttercream. They are delicious made with or without pecan nuts.

Ingredients:

50g (2oz) pecan nuts (optional)

100g (4oz) butter, softened

50g (2oz) soft light brown sugar

100g (4oz) self-raising flour

2 medium eggs

6 tablespoons maple syrup

For the buttercream:

100g (4oz) butter, softened

225g (8oz) icing sugar

1 tablespoon warm water

$1/2$ teaspoon vanilla essence

You will also need:

a 12-hole shallow bun tray

12 paper cupcake cases

❄ Makes 12 cupcakes.

If you are adding pecan nuts, put them in a plastic food bag and seal the end. Crush them into small pieces with a rolling pin.

1 Heat the oven to 190°C, 375°F or gas mark 5. Beat the butter and sugar in a large bowl until they are light and fluffy. Sift in the flour.

2 Beat the eggs in a cup. Add them to the bowl, with the nuts and maple syrup. Stir until everything is well mixed.

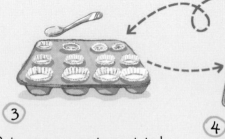

3 Put a paper case in each hole in the tray. Use a teaspoon to divide the mixture between the paper cases. Bake for 12-15 minutes until risen and firm.

4 Leave in the tray for a few minutes. Lift each one onto a wire rack to cool. Meanwhile, make the buttercream.

5 Beat the butter, icing sugar, warm water and vanilla together in a bowl until smooth. Spread some over each cake, when it is cool.

These will keep
for up to 5 days
in an airtight
container.

You could decorate your
cupcakes with nuts, sweets
or sprinkles. Make different
colours of topping, by adding
one or two drops of food dye
to the buttercream.

33

Lebkuchen

These German biscuits have a soft, chewy texture and a spicy flavour.
Traditionally, they are round and covered with a very thin layer of icing, but you
can often find them in other shapes, such as hearts.

Ingredients:

65g (2$\frac{1}{2}$oz) plain flour

$\frac{1}{2}$ teaspoon baking powder

$\frac{1}{2}$ teaspoon cinnamon

1 teaspoon ground mixed spice

75g (3oz) soft light brown sugar

50g (2oz) ground almonds

2 medium eggs

3 soft dates

50g (2oz) marzipan

3 tablespoons smooth apricot jam

50g (2oz) chopped mixed peel

100g (4oz) whole blanched almonds

For the icing:

25g (1oz) icing sugar

2 teaspoons water

❄ Makes around 12 biscuits.

① Put the flour, baking powder, cinnamon and mixed spice in a large bowl. Stir in the sugar and ground almonds.

② Break the eggs into a cup or a small bowl and beat them with a fork. Cut the dates in half. Take out the stones if there are any.

③ Put the dates in another large bowl and mash them with a fork. Mix 1 tablespoon of egg into the dates.

④ Crumble the marzipan into the date mixture. Add the jam and mash everything together.

⑤ Stir in the rest of the eggs, a little at a time. Add the mixed peel and the floury mixture. Mix everything together well.

6

Cover the bowl with plastic foodwrap and put it in the fridge for 30 minutes. Heat the oven to 160°C, 325°F or gas mark 3.

Space well apart.

7

Line two baking trays. Use a dessertspoon to drop round blobs of the mixture onto the trays. Arrange 3 almonds on top of each blob.

8

Bake for 15 minutes until lightly browned. Leave on the trays for 5 minutes, then put on a wire rack to cool.

9

For the icing, sift the icing sugar into a bowl. Stir in the water. Brush over the biscuits.

These will keep for up to 5 days in an airtight container.

The glaze on these biscuits is so thin, you can hardly see it.

Chocolate Christmas cake

This rich chocolate orange cake is packed with nuts. If you don't like dried fruits, this makes a delicious alternative to traditional Christmas fruit cake.

Ingredients:

1 large orange

225g (8oz) plain chocolate

350g (12oz) unsalted almonds, hazelnuts and walnuts, preferably ready-chopped

200g (7oz) caster sugar

25g (1oz) butter

5 large eggs

You will also need:

a 20cm (8in) tin with a loose base

If you can't get ready-chopped nuts, put whole nuts in a plastic food bag and seal the end. Crush them into small pieces with a rolling pin.

1

Heat the oven to 180°C, 350°F or gas mark 4. Grease and line the tin. Grate the zest from the orange and squeeze out the juice.

2

Cut the chocolate into small pieces. Put the chocolate, zest, nuts and sugar into a large bowl.

3

Heat the butter in a pan until it melts. Turn off the heat and add the orange juice. Add the buttery mixture to the ingredients in the bowl. Stir everything together.

4

Separate the eggs. Put the whites into a large, clean bowl. Add the yolks to the chocolate mixture and stir them in.

This will keep for up to a week, covered with foil or foodwrap.

5

Whisk the egg whites until they are really thick. When you lift up the whisk, they should make stiff peaks, like this.

6

Add two large spoonfuls of egg white to the chocolate mixture. Use a metal spoon to fold them in gently. Add the rest of the whites and fold them in.

7

Spoon the mixture into the tin. Bake the cake for one hour.

Peel off the parchment.

8

Push a skewer into the middle of the cake. When it comes out without cake mixture stuck to it, it is ready. Leave it in the tin for 10 minutes, then turn it onto a wire rack.

You could sift icing sugar over your cake in a doily pattern. See page 44 to find out how.

Gingerbread houses

Making houses out of gingerbread is a tradition that began in Germany, inspired by the gingerbread house in the fairy tale 'Hansel and Gretel'. You can use any sweets, sprinkles, or other decorations on your gingerbread houses.

Ingredients:

350g (12oz) plain flour

1¹/₂ teaspoons ground ginger

¹/₂ teaspoon ground cinnamon

1 teaspoon bicarbonate of soda

100g (4oz) butter, chilled

175g (6oz) light muscovado sugar

1 medium egg

2 tablespoons golden syrup

writing icing, sweets and sprinkles for decorating

❄ Makes around 10 houses.

① Heat the oven to 180°C, 350°F or gas mark 4. Line two baking trays. Mix the flour, ginger, cinnamon and bicarbonate of soda in a large bowl.

② Cut the butter into chunks. Rub it into the flour until the mixture looks like breadcrumbs. Stir in the sugar.

③ Break the egg into a small bowl and mix in the syrup. Add it to the flour. Stir everything together, then squeeze it into a smooth dough.

Dust a rolling pin and surface with flour.

④ Roll out the dough, until it is as thick as your little finger.

⑤ Cut off the wobbly edges with a sharp knife, to make a square. Then, cut the square into four pieces, like this.

⑥ Cut each piece in half, to make a rectangle. Then, cut a triangle from the top corners of each rectangle, to make house shapes.

⑦ Squeeze the scraps into a ball, roll it out and cut more houses. Put them onto the trays. Bake for 12-15 minutes until dark golden.

⑧ Leave the houses on the trays for a few minutes, then put on a wire rack to cool. Decorate with writing icing and press on sweets and sprinkles.

These will keep for up to 5 days in an airtight container.

You could cover a whole biscuit with icing (see page 44 for the icing recipe). Leave the icing to dry, then draw on top with writing icing.

Stollen

This fruit bread has a marzipan filling, which represents the baby Jesus wrapped in blankets. It has been eaten at Christmas in Germany for over 500 years.

Ingredients:

1 lemon

50g (2oz) glacé cherries

50g (2oz) almonds

350g (12oz) strong white bread flour

1 teaspoon salt

1 teaspoon ground mixed spice

40g (1½oz) caster sugar

2 teaspoons fast action yeast

100g (4oz) mixture of currants, raisins and sultanas

25g (1oz) chopped mixed peel

50g (2oz) butter

200ml (7fl oz) milk

For the marzipan filling:

1 medium egg

65g (2½oz) caster sugar

65g (2½oz) ground almonds

1 Grate the zest from the lemon. Cut the cherries and almonds into small pieces. Put them into a large bowl with the zest.

2 Put the flour, salt, mixed spice, sugar, yeast, dried fruit and peel into the large bowl. Mix them together.

3 Put the butter and half the milk in a pan. Heat gently until the butter has just melted. Take off the heat, then add the rest of the milk.

4 Pour the milky mixture into the bowl. Stir to make a dough.

5 To knead the dough, follow steps 4 and 5 on page 28. Then, press the dough into an oblong shape, about 25 x 20cm (10 x 8in).

6 For the filling, break the egg into a bowl. Stir in the sugar and ground almonds. Spread it down the middle of the dough.

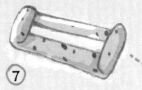

7 Fold in the two shorter edges over the filling. Then fold over one long edge, then the other.

8 Lift onto a greased baking tray with the join facing down.

9 Cover with a clean tea towel. Leave in a warm place for 1-2 hours until it has risen to twice its original size.

10 Heat the oven to 180°C, 350°F or gas mark 4. Remove the tea towel. Cover with baking parchment and bake for 35-40 minutes until lightly browned.

11 Leave on a wire rack for a few minutes to cool. You could sift icing sugar over the top.

You could use 200g (7oz) of bought marzipan, instead of making your own. Roll into a sausage around 23cm (9in) long. In step 6, place it down the middle of the dough.

This will keep for up to 5 days in an airtight container.

Toppings and fillings

You could use this whipped cream to make the raspberry cream filling for the Christmas log. Or try the orange cream or chestnut cream instead. The buttercream is for decorating the maple syrup cupcakes or the Christmas log, and the mincemeat is to fill the mince pies.

Whipped cream

① Pour some whipping cream into a bowl. Hold the bowl in one hand. Use your other hand to move the whisk quickly around and around the bowl.

② Carry on until the cream starts to form stiff peaks when you lift the whisk, but stop before it becomes too solid.

Orange cream

Grate the zest from an orange. Put it in a bowl with 250g (9oz) mascarpone. Sift over 25g (1oz) icing sugar. Mix everything together.

Chestnut cream

Put 250g (9oz) chestnut purée, from a tin or tube, into a bowl. Beat with a fork. Whip 200ml (7fl oz) cream, then stir it into the purée. Contains nuts.

Buttercream

100g (4oz) butter, softened
  (or dairy-free spread)
225g (8oz) icing sugar
1 tablespoon warm water
1/2 teaspoon vanilla essence

① Beat the butter with a wooden spoon until it is soft and creamy. Sift over about a third of the sugar. Stir it in.

② Sift over the rest of the sugar. Add the water and vanilla essence. Beat everything until it is pale and fluffy.

For coloured buttercream, pour 1-2 drops of food dye onto a teaspoon. Stir them in after you have beaten the buttercream.

For chocolate buttercream, mix 1 tablespoon of cocoa with the water. Add it to the mixture at step 2.

Mincemeat

If you are allergic to nuts, just leave them out.

1 orange
1 lemon
75g (3oz) seedless grapes
25g (1oz) hazelnuts

1 apple
150g (5oz) raisins
ground cinnamon,
  nutmeg and ginger

① Grate the zest from the orange and lemon. Chop the grapes and hazelnuts into small pieces.

② Don't bother peeling the apple. Use the large holes of the grater to grate it. Stop when you get to the core.

③ Put the zest, grapes, nuts and apple in a bowl. Stir in the raisins and a pinch each of cinnamon, nutmeg and ginger.

43

Decorating ideas

There are lots of different ways you can decorate your cakes and biscuits. Here are some ideas for different types of icing, sugar patterns and marzipan decorations.

Icing

175g (6oz) icing sugar

1¹/₂ tablespoons warm water

(Or follow the quantities in the recipe you are using.)

① Sift the icing sugar into a bowl. Stir in the warm water to make a smooth paste.

② Use a teaspoon to scoop up some icing and spread it onto a cake or biscuit. For a smooth surface, dip a blunt knife into some warm water and slide it over the icing.

Coloured icing

For coloured icing, measure 1 or 2 drops of food dye onto a teaspoon, then stir it into the icing. Add more for a darker colour.

Lemon icing

For lemon icing, replace the water with 1¹/₂ tablespoons of lemon juice. Or use orange or clementine juice instead.

Doily designs

Lay a doily over a cake. Sift icing sugar or cocoa over it. Then, carefully lift off the doily.

Stencil patterns

① Take a piece of paper that's bigger than your cake. Fold it in half. Draw half a shape against the fold. Cut it out.

② Unfold the paper and lay it over your cake. Sift a little icing sugar or cocoa over it. Carefully lift off the stencil.

You could also use the cut-out shape from the middle of your stencil, like this.

Home-made sugar sprinkles

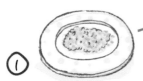

① Put 1 tablespoon of granulated sugar onto a plate. Add 1 or 2 drops of food dye and mix it in. Spread it onto a plate to dry.

② Use the back of a spoon to break up the sugar. Then, scoop it up and sprinkle it onto an iced cake.

You could use a stencil with some sugar sprinkles, too.

Marzipan shapes

① Put some 'white' marzipan into a bowl. Make a hollow in it and drop in 1 or 2 drops of food dye.

② Fold the marzipan over the dye. Use your hands to mix it until it is evenly coloured.

You could make shapes from coloured ready-to-roll icing instead of marzipan.

③ Put the marzipan onto a clean surface. Roll it out with a rolling pin. Use cookie cutters to cut out the shapes you want.

For candy canes, roll out two sticks of red and white marzipan. Twist them together, roll again, then shape into a cane.

You could make a lattice design with writing icing and stick on sweets.

Wrapping ideas

Biscuits and cakes can make perfect Christmas presents. You could put them in a wrapped food box or tin, or try out the pretty packaging ideas below.

Some of the recipes in this book keep better than others. Check the recipe to find out how long you can keep each thing, and the best way to store it.

Jar lid cover

① Find a plate or saucer around 5cm (2in) wider than your jar lid. Put the plate on some decorated paper or material and draw around it. Then, cut it out.

② Put it over the jar lid. Press the edges down over the lid and secure it with a rubber band. Then tie some pretty ribbon or thread around it.

Muffin cases

① For each muffin, cut a square of baking parchment around 13cm (5in) across. Lay it over a hole in a muffin tray. Push it in, squashing until it fits.

② Spoon in the muffin mix and bake. When your muffins have cooled, you could tie some ribbon or thread around them.

Index

Additional design and cover by Nancy Leschnikoff

Photography by Howard Allman
Edited by Abigail Wheatley and Jane Chisholm   Art Director: Mary Cartwright
Food preparation by Dagmar Vesely, Abigail Wheatley and Nelupa Hussain   Digital imaging: Nick Wakeford
Every effort has been made to trace the copyright holders of material in this book. If any rights have been omitted,
the publishers offer to rectify this in any subsequent editions following notification.